Copyright © 2025

All rights reserved. This book, including its ideas, structure, and original content, is protected by copyright law. No portion of this publication may be reproduced, distributed, or transmitted in any form or by any means—whether electronic, mechanical, photocopying, recording, or otherwise—without prior written permission from the author, except in the case of brief quotations used for reviews, educational reference, or critical analysis.

This work represents the author's original thought, expression, and creative effort. Any unauthorized use, adaptation, or appropriation of the material is strictly prohibited and may result in legal action.

Chapter 1 — The Speed Illusion: Seeing Beyond Momentum

In an age obsessed with acceleration, "moving fast" has become a badge of honor. We rush through tasks, scroll through endless updates, and measure our worth by the pace of our progress. Yet beneath the surface of this relentless motion lies a quiet illusion — that speed itself equals significance. The truth is subtler: sometimes, the faster we move, the less we see. The more we push, the less we grow. This chapter explores the hidden costs of the cult of urgency, the quiet power of depth, and the art of reclaiming your personal rhythm in a world that mistakes movement for meaning.

1.1 – The Cult of Urgency

There's a cultural myth that says: *if you're not moving fast, you're falling behind.* It's the quiet pressure behind your morning anxiety, the guilt you feel for taking a day off, the restless compulsion to fill every silence with productivity. Urgency has become an identity — a socially sanctioned addiction disguised as ambition.

But beneath this craving for momentum lies something deeper and more vulnerable: **the fear of stillness.**

Stillness confronts us with ourselves. When we stop, we hear the echoes of our own doubts — the questions about who we are when we're not performing. The need to rush, therefore, often masks discomfort with reflection. The busyness feels safer than awareness. The to-do list becomes a shield against the possibility of discovering that we're unsure, lonely, or unsatisfied.

In this way, **urgency becomes emotional armor.** We wear it to avoid vulnerability. Every quick reply, every multitasked hour, every restless project is a small declaration: *I'm still moving, I must still matter.*

But the paradox is that constant urgency actually distances us from the very things we think we're chasing — meaning, purpose, clarity, and peace. The more we rush, the shallower our attention becomes. We trade presence for progress, depth for distraction. We start living in the future tense — always anticipating the next thing rather than experiencing the current one.

If urgency is a cult, then its rituals are everywhere: inboxes, notifications, deadlines, metrics, updates, and goals. We rarely question them because they've been woven into our sense of worth. But liberation begins when we pause long enough to see that "fast" isn't always "forward." What we truly crave isn't speed — it's significance.

The Inner Beliefs Behind Urgency

Ask yourself: *Why do I rush?*
There are usually hidden beliefs at play. You might fear missing out, disappointing someone, or seeming lazy. You might equate stillness with stagnation. Or perhaps deep down, you're afraid that if you slow down, you'll discover emptiness beneath your momentum.

But none of these fears are facts. They're stories. And stories can be rewritten.

The first step toward escaping the cult of urgency is recognizing that you have a choice. You can honor your natural pace. You can protect your attention. You can measure success not by how much you do, but by how aligned your actions feel with your values.

Speed can serve you — but only when you are the one choosing the gear.

Exercise: The Decision Reflection

Write about the last time you rushed into a decision.

Maybe it was accepting an offer, sending a message, buying something, or committing to a plan. Recall the moment in detail — the feeling in your body, the thoughts in your mind.

Now answer these questions:

1. What belief drove that speed? (e.g., "If I don't act now, I'll lose my chance.")
2. What emotion was I avoiding by acting quickly? (e.g., uncertainty, doubt, or fear.)
3. What might have changed if I had waited?

This exercise isn't about regret. It's about awareness. When you identify the belief behind your urgency, you loosen its grip. You begin to replace reaction with reflection — and that is where real mastery begins.

1.2 – What It Means to Go Deep Instead of Fast

Speed creates the illusion of growth. Depth creates the reality of it.

To "go deep" means to give your full attention to a single pursuit, person, or question. It's not about working harder or longer; it's about **working from a place of presence and curiosity**. Depth is what transforms effort into understanding. It's what turns repetition into mastery.

But depth demands patience. It refuses to be rushed. In a world trained to seek novelty, the practice of depth feels almost rebellious. It asks you to stay with something long enough to become intimate with its details — to move beyond the surface layer of gratification and into the quiet satisfaction of true progress.

The Hidden Power of Depth

Depth rewires your relationship with time. Instead of seeing hours as units to spend, you begin to see them as containers for experience. Ten minutes of deep engagement can be more transformative than ten hours of scattered busyness.

Depth also changes your relationship with yourself. The longer you stay with something — whether it's a craft, a friendship, or a self-inquiry — the more you discover about your own patterns of resistance, your triggers, your strengths, and your tendencies to give up or push too hard. Depth turns every pursuit into a mirror for self-knowledge.

Think of the difference between sprinting across a landscape and walking through it slowly. The sprinter covers more ground, but the walker sees more detail. The sprinter knows where they went; the walker knows where they are.

In life, we often mistake "covering ground" for "making progress." But covering ground only takes you somewhere new. Depth takes you somewhere *real*.

Depth vs. Pace: Rethinking Progress

Fast progress is often visible. It produces numbers, achievements, and applause. Deep progress is quieter. It shows up as confidence, clarity, or emotional resilience — things that can't be measured but can be felt.

The challenge is that deep progress can feel like stagnation. When you're digging into something complex — learning a skill, healing a wound, developing emotional intelligence — the growth curve often looks flat. But this is an illusion too. Just as a seed grows roots before it grows leaves, depth begins in the unseen layers.

If you learn to trust the unseen work, you become unstoppable. Because depth anchors you. It keeps your sense of worth independent of outcomes. You stop chasing validation and start pursuing truth.

Reflection Prompt: The Slow Growth Audit

Take a few minutes to reflect on this:

Identify one area of your life where slower progress might actually mean deeper growth.

Maybe it's your career, where you could focus on mastering your craft instead of chasing the next promotion.
Maybe it's your relationships, where slowing down might mean truly listening instead of reacting.

Maybe it's your self-development, where giving yourself time to integrate lessons is more valuable than rushing to "fix" yourself.

Write down your reflections. Then ask:

- What would it look like to prioritize depth here?
- What habits or expectations would I need to release?
- How would my daily choices change if I trusted slow growth?

Depth is not about doing less — it's about doing what matters most, with your whole attention.

1.3 – Reclaiming Your Personal Rhythm

Every living thing has a rhythm — tides, seasons, heartbeats, breaths. You do too. The problem is, modern life rarely honors it. We live by external clocks: deadlines, schedules, notifications, expectations. Over time, this disconnect from our inner tempo leaves us burnt out, anxious, and creatively depleted.

Reclaiming your rhythm means **rediscovering your natural flow of energy, focus, and rest.** It's the process of learning when to move, when to pause, and when to renew. It's not about balance in the abstract sense — it's about *harmony*.

When you find your rhythm, work becomes more sustainable. Rest becomes more restorative. Creativity begins to emerge naturally instead of being forced. You start to notice patterns: when you're most alert, when you need solitude, when inspiration tends to strike.

Listening to Your Inner Tempo

To reclaim your rhythm, you must first become a careful observer of yourself. Ask:

- When during the day do I feel most alive or focused?
- When does my body crave rest?

- What environments energize me, and which drain me?

These questions are deceptively simple but deeply revealing. The answers can help you design your life around your natural energy rather than fighting against it.

Most of us try to "manage time." But time is fixed; energy is flexible. **Energy management is the new time management.** If you align your most meaningful tasks with your peak energy windows, you'll do better work with less strain. If you honor your lows with genuine rest instead of guilt, your highs become more powerful.

The Rhythm of Renewal

Rhythm is not only about work — it's about recovery. Without rest, rhythm collapses into noise. Renewal can take many forms: solitude, play, nature, stillness, art, prayer, or movement. What matters is that it reconnects you to something unhurried.

Imagine your life as music. Without pauses, there's no melody — just chaos. Rest isn't the absence of productivity; it's the punctuation that gives your life structure and meaning. The art of rhythm lies in knowing when to play and when to pause.

Practical Tool: Create Your Tempo Map

A **tempo map** is a simple yet powerful visual tool for reclaiming your rhythm. Here's how to make one:

1. **Draw a seven-day grid.** Across the top, write the days of the week. Down the side, mark the hours or time blocks (morning, midday, afternoon, evening, night).
2. **Track your energy and mood for one week.**
   Every few hours, note your energy level on a scale from 1–10 and jot down what you were doing. Also record your emotional tone (e.g., calm, inspired, tense, drained).

3. **Look for patterns.**
   After a week, you'll begin to see rhythms emerge. Maybe your focus peaks mid-morning and dips mid-afternoon. Maybe you're more creative in the evening or more social on Fridays.
4. **Design around your energy, not the clock.**
   - Schedule deep or demanding work during your high-energy windows.
   - Use your low points for reflection, light tasks, or rest.
   - Protect your renewal rituals — make them non-negotiable.
5. **Adjust and revisit weekly.**
   Your rhythm will evolve as your responsibilities and seasons of life change. The goal isn't rigidity — it's responsiveness.

By mapping your tempo, you begin to see yourself not as a machine to be optimized, but as an organism to be understood. You become the conductor of your own symphony, rather than a musician playing someone else's tune.

The Deeper Message of Rhythm

When you live at your own rhythm, you reclaim something far greater than time — you reclaim your autonomy. You stop letting the world dictate your pace. You learn that success doesn't come from how fast you go, but from how fully you inhabit each step.

In stillness, you remember what truly matters.
In slowness, you discover the richness of attention.
In rhythm, you rediscover yourself.

Conclusion: Beyond the Speed Illusion

The world often confuses speed with purpose. But momentum without meaning is just motion — and motion alone can't fulfill you. The illusion of speed is that it makes you feel alive while quietly exhausting your spirit.

To see beyond momentum is to recognize that life's deepest work happens at a human pace — slow enough to feel, patient enough to learn, humble enough to grow. When you honor that pace, urgency loses its grip. You stop sprinting toward the future and begin walking steadily through the present, awake to the texture of your own experience.

The next chapters will build upon this foundation — exploring how to cultivate resilience, creativity, and authentic direction in a world that constantly pulls you toward haste. But for now, pause. Breathe. Ask yourself:

What might emerge in your life if you finally allowed yourself to go slower — and go deeper?

Chapter 2 — "The Architecture of Effort: Building a Life That Scales"

There is a quiet truth about progress that few people talk about: it's not powered by constant hustle, heroic bursts of willpower, or relentless self-control. It's built—brick by brick—through structure. Behind every life that grows sustainably is an invisible architecture: a network of habits, boundaries, and systems that catch you when motivation slips and hold you when the world shakes.

To "scale" one's life doesn't mean to do more, faster. It means to grow with stability, to evolve without collapsing under your own ambitions. It's the art of building an ecosystem where your energy, attention, and time compound instead of depleting.

This chapter explores that architecture. We'll move from the mechanics of sustainability to the emotional wisdom of discipline, and finally to the creative power of constraints. Together, these ideas form a blueprint—not for perfection, but for endurance with grace.

2.1 – Designing for Sustainability

Willpower is a wonderful spark, but a terrible engine. It ignites the beginning of change, yet burns out quickly when asked to power the whole journey. The people who sustain effort over years don't rely on being stronger or more determined—they build systems that make consistency easier than inconsistency.

A system is any pattern of actions, environments, and expectations that reduces friction toward a goal. It's the difference between waking up hoping you'll feel like exercising and simply showing up because your shoes are by the door, your playlist is ready, and your workout starts when your morning tea finishes steeping.

Sustainability, in this sense, is not a moral victory—it's a design choice.

The Physics of Effort

Every action in life has a cost: mental energy, decision fatigue, emotional resistance. Systems distribute that cost more evenly across time. Instead of asking yourself to climb a mountain each morning, you build a staircase—small, repeatable steps that get you there without breaking your spirit.

Sustainability means designing the path so that success is not a daily miracle but an ordinary event. The more friction you remove from doing the right thing, the more likely it becomes your default.

Consider how architects build cities: they anticipate movement. Sidewalks appear where people tend to walk; lighting follows the flow of use. A sustainable life follows the same principle—shape your environment around your real behavior, not your idealized self. If you keep missing your meditation time, maybe it's not discipline that's missing—it's placement, timing, or the cue that reminds you to start.

Energy Management vs. Time Management

Most of us design our days around time, but energy is the true currency of effort. You can always borrow time by sleeping less or multitasking, but when energy runs out, even the smallest task feels impossible. Sustainability is therefore about managing energy cycles—knowing when you are best at focus, reflection, or rest— and matching the right work to the right rhythm.

Ask yourself: What kind of energy does this task require, and when do I have it?

This question turns productivity into alignment. You stop fighting your nature and start collaborating with it. That's how effort becomes lighter—not by working less, but by working *with* yourself.

Exercise: Design One Sustainable System

Sketch a small system that supports one of your ongoing goals.
It could be as simple as:

- **Goal:** Write daily.
  System: Keep a notebook on the breakfast table. No phone until you've written one paragraph.
- **Goal:** Eat healthier.
  System: Prepare a "default lunch" every Sunday—something you enjoy enough not to crave takeout.
- **Goal:** Stay in touch with friends.
  System: Set a monthly reminder to send one thoughtful message.

The power of this exercise is in noticing how design reduces decision-making. When your systems are aligned with your values, you stop negotiating with yourself every day—and that is the essence of sustainability.

2.2 – Discipline as Compassion

For many people, the word *discipline* evokes a kind of inner rigidity—rules, self-denial, punishment for imperfection. But this is a tragic misunderstanding. Discipline, when rightly understood, is not about control; it's about care.

True discipline is a love language directed toward your future self. It's how you protect what matters most from the whims of the moment. It's how you create the conditions in which your potential can safely unfold.

From Punishment to Protection

Imagine a parent teaching a child to cross the street. The parent doesn't grab the child's hand out of anger, but out of love—knowing that boundaries ensure freedom later. Discipline is the adult version of that gesture: setting limits not because you mistrust yourself, but because you value yourself enough to make safety non-negotiable.

When discipline arises from compassion, it transforms. Waking up early becomes a gift of quiet time rather than a badge of toughness. Saying "no" to distractions becomes an act of loyalty to your deepest priorities.

You begin to see that every rule you create—sleeping enough, budgeting wisely, maintaining boundaries—says, *I believe my future deserves to be healthy, peaceful, and alive.*

The Emotional Architecture of Effort

Compassionate discipline recognizes that effort has emotional weather. Some days are clear, others are stormy. When you expect consistency from yourself as though you were a machine, you break the human spirit that effort depends on. Sustainable discipline bends like a tree—it adjusts, forgives, and returns to form.

This is where many self-improvement journeys fail: they confuse consistency with perfection. Compassionate discipline accepts variability as part of rhythm. Missing a day doesn't mean failure; it means the system needs more flexibility or better recovery time.

If you treat discipline as care, relapse becomes feedback, not shame. And feedback is how every living system evolves.

Reflection Prompt: Rules as Invitations

Reflect on one "rule" you've set for yourself—maybe about fitness, work, or relationships.
Now ask: *Is this rule an invitation to care for my future self, or is it a punishment for my past self?*

Rewrite the rule if necessary so it feels nurturing, not punitive.

For example:

- Instead of "I must stop wasting time on my phone," reframe it as "I want to give my mind more room to breathe."
- Instead of "I can't eat sugar," try "I choose foods that make my body feel calm and clear."
- Instead of "I must be productive every day," say "I create space for both effort and restoration."

This small linguistic shift changes how discipline feels—and therefore, how long it lasts. Compassion turns effort into devotion.

2.3 – The Art of Constructive Constraint

We live in an age that worships boundless possibility. We are told to "dream bigger," "say yes," "do it all." Yet, strangely, many of us feel overwhelmed, scattered, and creatively paralyzed. The problem isn't too little freedom—it's too much.

Constraints, far from limiting us, are the scaffolds that make meaningful work possible. They narrow chaos into clarity. They turn formless desire into directed energy.

Freedom Through Boundaries

Think of an artist facing a blank canvas. The vastness of "anything" is intimidating. But once the artist chooses a color palette, a theme, a medium—creativity awakens. The same is true in life: when you decide what *not* to do, what remains gains power and focus.

Voluntary constraints—time boxes, budget limits, digital fasts, or creative parameters—create a container for expression. They are not cages but vessels.

Paradoxically, boundaries expand freedom because they make it usable. Like the banks of a river, they give flow its form.

Constraint as Catalyst

Every resource you lack forces you to innovate. Every rule you impose clarifies your values. When you intentionally limit options, you train your mind to deepen rather than widen—to find new possibilities within the frame you've chosen.

For example:

- Setting a **time constraint** (one hour to write, no editing) often leads to more authentic output than endless tinkering.
- A **budget constraint** can sharpen creativity in problem-solving and decision-making.
- A **digital fast** can rekindle attention, revealing how much energy was leaking into distraction.

Constraints teach efficiency, but they also teach humility. They remind us that mastery isn't about infinite expansion—it's about the elegance of working well within limits.

Practice: Choose One Constructive Constraint

Pick one voluntary limit to experiment with for a week. Examples include:

- A **time box:** "I'll stop working at 6 p.m., no matter what."
- An **input limit:** "I'll read only one article per day instead of endlessly scrolling."
- A **digital fast:** "I'll leave my phone in another room during meals."

At the end of the week, record what you noticed. Did the constraint make you more focused, relaxed, or inventive? Did it reveal hidden dependencies or free up mental space?

You may discover that limits don't restrict you—they refine you.

Building a Life That Scales

The architecture of effort is built from these three principles: sustainability, compassion, and constraint. Together, they form a structure strong enough to hold growth without collapse.

A scalable life is not one that does *more*—it's one that sustains meaning as it grows. It's the difference between building a ladder that endlessly extends upward and building a foundation that can carry weight across time.

Integration: The Systemic Mindset

To build a life that scales:

1. **Design for sustainability**—replace willpower with structure.
2. **Anchor discipline in compassion**—let your boundaries express care, not control.
3. **Use constructive constraints**—choose limits that sharpen your focus and creativity.

These elements reinforce each other. Systems reduce the burden on discipline; compassionate discipline makes systems humane; constraints make both manageable.

The Long View

Scaling your life is not about optimizing every minute—it's about ensuring that effort today doesn't destroy capacity tomorrow. Sustainability without compassion becomes rigidity. Compassion without systems becomes sentiment. Systems without constraints become sprawl.

The mature form of effort is architectural: planned, balanced, and capable of withstanding time's weather.

Think of your life as a cathedral under construction. Each small brick—a habit, a morning ritual, a boundary—is laid patiently, not to finish quickly, but to endure beautifully. The scaffolding may change, but the purpose remains: to create a space within yourself where meaning can echo for decades.

Final Reflection: Building for the Future You

Ask yourself:

- What would it mean to build a life I can *inhabit* comfortably, not just achieve within?

- Which parts of my effort today feel like architecture—and which still feel like improvisation?
- How can I replace the fragile motivation of the moment with durable design?

The answers won't come all at once. But each system you create, each compassionate rule you rewrite, each boundary you honor—these are the blueprints of a scalable life.

Effort, in the end, is not about striving harder but building wiser.

When you design your days as an architect designs structures—considering load, flow, and resilience—you discover that the secret to lasting progress isn't speed or intensity. It's design that honors both the builder and the building.

And that's how your life begins to scale—not by expanding endlessly outward, but by deepening gracefully inward, creating a rhythm of effort that can last a lifetime.

Chapter 3 — Inner Velocity: The Physics of Meaning

We often describe life in the language of movement — we "make progress," "find direction," or "lose momentum." But few of us stop to ask: *what actually moves us?*

Speed without alignment can exhaust us, yet stillness with clarity can hold more energy than chaos in motion. "Inner Velocity" is about reclaiming that movement — the steady, self-generated force that comes from being internally aligned with what truly matters.

Just as in physics, every form of motion has a cause, a resistance, and a center of gravity. Likewise, meaningful lives move through three universal dynamics: **the momentum of purpose**, **the friction of feedback**, and **the gravity of values**. Together, they form the invisible mechanics of fulfillment — a kind of "inner physics" that governs why we keep going, where we get stuck, and what we revolve around.

3.1 – Momentum of Purpose

The Physics of Small Alignment

In physics, momentum is the product of mass and velocity — the more mass something has, or the faster it moves, the harder it is to stop. In life, *purpose* works the same way. When your actions align with something meaningful, each step, however small, compounds into momentum. Over time, it becomes difficult to stop moving in that direction — not because of willpower, but because of resonance.

The misconception about purpose is that it arrives in grand revelations or singular missions. But most of the time, it begins quietly — through the repetition of small, aligned actions that reinforce who you're becoming. Writing one paragraph a day, checking in with a friend each week, taking time each morning to breathe before reacting — these are not minor gestures. They are momentum builders.

When you move consistently in a direction that feels authentic, you begin to experience what might be called *inner velocity*: a state where action feels natural, and time feels less like a battle and more like flow. Purpose then becomes less of a *destination* and more of a *vector* — not something you chase, but something that propels you.

Alignment Over Achievement

Achievement can be deceptive. It gives the appearance of forward motion — promotions, milestones, recognition — but without alignment, those achievements are like wheels spinning in sand. Purposeful momentum, on the other hand, doesn't depend on external speed. It's a deepening movement rather than an accelerating one.

Ask yourself: do your daily actions reinforce your sense of meaning, or simply your sense of movement? You may find that what drains you most is not effort, but misalignment — running hard in a direction you don't actually wish to go.

A simple truth hides in this paradox: it takes less energy to move in the right direction, even if that direction requires effort. Purpose creates efficiency because it channels your limited attention into coherent flow. The more aligned your actions, the less friction you experience internally, and the more momentum you generate.

Exercise: The Direction Statement

Instead of asking, "What do I want to achieve?" try asking, "What moves me?" The first question seeks control; the second seeks truth.

Exercise:
Write a *Direction Statement* — a brief declaration that captures what moves you, not where you're trying to go. Keep it under 50 words.

Here's a simple framework to guide you:

"I feel most alive when I am ___, because it helps me ___."

For example:

- "I feel most alive when I am learning and sharing insights, because it helps me understand and connect with others."
- "I feel most alive when I am designing solutions that bring clarity, because it helps me reduce chaos and increase harmony."

Your direction statement isn't a goal; it's a compass. Goals can expire — your direction can evolve, but it remains centered in what energizes you. Once you have it, evaluate your weekly actions through this lens: *Does this move me in the direction of aliveness, or away from it?*

Momentum of purpose begins not with speed, but with this clarity.

3.2 – Friction as Feedback

Resistance as Signal

In motion, friction is the force that resists movement. It slows things down, generates heat, and can even halt progress. But in physics, friction also makes motion possible. Without friction, you can't walk — your feet would just slide endlessly without traction. The same paradox applies to personal growth: the resistance you encounter isn't always a barrier; sometimes it's the texture that allows you to gain grip.

Every meaningful pursuit introduces friction — fatigue, doubt, setbacks, discomfort. Most of us interpret these sensations as signs that something is wrong, but often they indicate that we're finally moving against inertia. The body feels sore not when it's failing, but when it's strengthening.

Resistance, therefore, is *data*. It can tell you whether you're misaligned, overextended, or evolving. The key is to learn to listen to what friction is saying instead of trying to eliminate it.

Types of Friction

1. **Friction of Misalignment**
   This kind of resistance feels draining and meaningless. You might be expending energy but feel emptier with each effort. It signals that your motion isn't aligned with your direction statement. When you feel this kind of friction, pause — your energy is likely being spent on a path that doesn't serve you.
2. **Friction of Growth**
   This friction feels uncomfortable but meaningful. It challenges you, stretches your limits, but also expands your sense of possibility. This is productive resistance — a sign that you're building capability and integrity.
3. **Friction of Integrity**
   Sometimes friction appears when your values and actions collide. You feel an inner dissonance, a subtle resistance that says, "Something here doesn't feel right." Listening to this form of friction often reveals where compromise has replaced conviction.

The Feedback Loop

Think of friction as feedback from the system of your life. When you encounter resistance, ask:

- Is this resistance protecting me or preparing me?
- Is it showing me a misalignment or a new edge of growth?

If you treat resistance as a teacher instead of an obstacle, every challenge becomes diagnostic — a way to refine your movement. This shift in perception transforms frustration into curiosity, and struggle into signal interpretation.

Reflection Prompt: When Was Resistance Trying to Teach You Something?

Take a few minutes to recall a recent situation where you faced persistent resistance. Maybe a project wouldn't progress, a relationship felt strained, or a personal habit kept breaking down. Instead of judging it, explore it through the following questions:

- What was the *message* hidden in that resistance?

- Was it pointing out a lack of clarity, a needed boundary, or a deeper value you ignored?
- If that friction had a voice, what would it say?

Write freely — don't analyze yet. Later, reread what you've written and underline any phrase that feels like guidance rather than complaint. That's your feedback loop revealing itself.

Over time, learning to decode resistance will become one of your most reliable forms of internal navigation.

3.3 – The Gravity of Values

The Invisible Center

In the physical universe, gravity is the force that organizes motion. Planets orbit stars because of gravitational pull. In human life, our *values* serve this same role — they are the invisible centers that shape our decisions, priorities, and relationships.

Without a gravitational center, movement becomes chaotic. You may chase multiple goals, adopt contradictory habits, or oscillate between directions. But once your values are clearly defined and consciously held, they create stability. You begin to make decisions not from impulse or fear, but from coherence.

Values are not moral slogans; they are gravitational truths. They define *what holds you together* when life's forces pull you in different directions.

Values as Decision Filters

Every choice you make either strengthens or weakens your orbit. When your actions align with your values, you stay in stable motion — consistent, energized, and purposeful. When they don't, you experience drift — that uneasy feeling of being slightly off-course, even when things look successful from the outside.

To use your values as a decision filter, start asking:

- Does this decision reflect who I want to be, or who I'm afraid to disappoint?
- Does it move me closer to integrity or merely closer to comfort?
- If I repeat this action daily, what kind of person will I become?

These questions bring gravity back into play. They prevent your life from spinning into scattered orbits of obligation.

Building Your Value Map

You can't navigate meaning without knowing your gravitational constants. The following tool — a *Value Map* — helps you visualize how your deepest principles influence your present goals.

Tool: The Value Map

Step 1: Identify Your Top Three Guiding Values

Think of values as *verbs*, not nouns. Instead of "honesty," try "speaking truth." Instead of "creativity," try "bringing new forms into the world." Values are living forces, not labels.

Ask yourself:

- When have I felt most at peace with my choices?
- What qualities was I expressing then?
- Which principles would I never want to betray, even under pressure?

Write your top three.

Example:

1. **Integrity** — staying true even when unseen.
2. **Growth** — becoming more capable and conscious.
3. **Connection** — building trust and empathy through shared experience.

Step 2: Connect Each Value to a Current Goal

For each value, link it to a current project, habit, or relationship. Describe how the value shapes your approach.

Example:

- *Integrity → Career choices:* I want to take on projects that match my beliefs, even if they pay less.
- *Growth → Health goal:* I'm exercising not to impress others, but to build consistency and self-respect.
- *Connection → Family:* I'm choosing to spend one evening a week in uninterrupted presence with loved ones.

Step 3: Identify Tensions and Realignments

Where are your values pulling against each other? Perhaps "growth" conflicts with "balance," or "creativity" competes with "stability." These tensions aren't flaws; they are gravitational interactions. Map them out. Then ask: *Which value should govern this particular orbit right now?*

Life's balance is dynamic — values take turns leading depending on context. The goal isn't perfect symmetry but conscious awareness.

Living Within Your Orbit

The more consistently you act in accordance with your values, the stronger their gravitational field becomes. Decision-making simplifies; anxiety reduces. You begin to feel an internal steadiness that doesn't depend on circumstance — a state we might call *equilibrium of meaning*.

And like planetary orbits, this equilibrium isn't static; it's dynamic stability. You'll still experience wobble, drift, and perturbation. But now, you'll recognize those fluctuations as part of a larger, balanced motion around a stable center — your values.

Integrating the Physics of Meaning

When we bring these three dynamics together — **momentum, friction, and gravity** — we get a fuller picture of how meaning moves within us.

- **Momentum of Purpose** gives us direction.
- **Friction as Feedback** gives us correction.
- **Gravity of Values** gives us coherence.

A purposeful life isn't one without resistance; it's one where resistance refines momentum and gravity holds it all together.

You might think of this as your personal physics equation:

Meaning = (Aligned Action × Reflection) ÷ Drift

Aligned action builds momentum. Reflection turns friction into feedback. Drift — the loss of clarity or integrity — weakens both. By regularly checking your direction, interpreting resistance, and anchoring to values, you sustain *inner velocity*.

Closing Reflection: The Steady Flame

Imagine a candle flame in a quiet room. Its light flickers, but its core remains steady. That's inner velocity — not the chaos of movement, but the constancy of purpose.

When your inner physics are aligned, even stillness contains momentum. You no longer chase speed; you *generate* motion from within. You stop asking, "How fast am I moving?" and start asking, "How true is my direction?"

This shift changes everything. It replaces restlessness with rhythm, exhaustion with endurance, and ambition with authenticity. You begin to live not as a body in perpetual motion, but as a mind in meaningful orbit.

Key Takeaways

1. **Momentum builds through small, aligned actions**, not grand leaps. Purpose compounds quietly.
2. **Friction is feedback.** Listen to what resistance teaches instead of fighting it.
3. **Values create gravity.** They keep your life from drifting into chaos and anchor your movement in meaning.
4. **Inner velocity is self-sustaining.** Once alignment, feedback, and values cohere, energy regenerates from within.
5. **Meaning is motion with coherence.** It's less about pace and more about direction, rhythm, and resonance.

Suggested Daily Practice

At the end of each day, ask three short questions:

1. What small action today built momentum in my direction?
2. What resistance today was trying to teach me?
3. Did I make at least one decision rooted in my values?

Answer honestly, briefly, and consistently. Over time, your responses will form a kind of logbook — a record of your inner velocity taking shape.

Chapter 4 — Creative Equilibrium: The Balance Between Chaos and Order

Creativity lives in paradox. It breathes in the space between discipline and freedom, between clarity and confusion, between what we can plan and what we can only discover. To live and create fully is to stand on the fertile edge of chaos—not to fall into disorder, but not to retreat into rigidity either. This chapter explores how to find, nurture, and sustain that edge.

Here, you'll learn that equilibrium is not about stillness. It's about responsiveness—a dance with life's unpredictability. The goal is not to eliminate chaos or impose total order, but to move gracefully between the two, finding rhythm in fluctuation.

4.1 – The Fertile Edge of Chaos

In nature, growth often happens at the edges—where the forest meets the field, where the tide touches the shore, where heat meets cold. These edges are unstable, but they're also rich with life. Creativity works the same way: it thrives at the boundaries between chaos and order.

When everything is predictable, there's comfort but little invention. When everything is disorderly, there's potential but little direction. The sweet spot lies between—the fertile edge where something new can emerge but still find form. This edge can feel uncomfortable because it resists both extremes. It asks us to trust in uncertainty without being consumed by it.

The Role of Uncertainty

Uncertainty often feels like danger. We crave clarity because it gives us control, and control gives us the illusion of safety. Yet, every major transformation in life—creative, personal, or professional—begins with some kind of disorientation. A painter faces a blank canvas. An entrepreneur faces a problem without a known solution. A person undergoing growth feels suspended between who they were and who they might become.

At first, this feels like chaos. But in truth, it's creation waiting to take form. The discomfort signals expansion. You're no longer anchored to the familiar; you're exploring a terrain that your old tools can't navigate. The chaos is not failure—it's the laboratory of the new self.

Finding the Bridge Across

When we stand at that edge, what carries us through is not certainty but connection. The "bridge" across chaos is built from small acts of trust—trust in process, in intuition, in time. Creativity isn't about leaping blindly into disorder; it's about learning to listen in the noise. The most resilient creators don't fight chaos—they work with it, shaping its raw material into something meaningful.

Bridges are built through habits of grounding—journaling, taking walks, speaking with mentors, or returning to a core purpose. These anchors don't erase chaos; they give us footing within it. Paradoxically, the steadier our inner foundation, the more freely we can explore disorder without losing ourselves in it.

Exercise: The Bridge Story

Think of a time when you felt lost, uncertain, or disoriented—perhaps a creative project that collapsed halfway, a career shift that shook your identity, or a relationship that forced you to redefine yourself.

Ask yourself:

- What part of me was dissolving during that time?
- What part of me was being born?
- What small habit, person, or insight acted as my bridge across the chaos?

Write about this moment not as a failure, but as a passage. What did you learn about your own creative rhythm—the way you navigate uncertainty? You may find that what seemed like collapse was actually the compost of renewal.

4.2 – Rituals of Renewal

If chaos is the wild terrain of creation, rituals are the cairns that mark our way through it. Rituals are not superstitions; they are intentional acts of rhythm. They remind us that growth requires both expansion and contraction, both work and rest, both risk and recovery.

Rituals offer coherence amid flux. They give creativity a container. The goal of ritual isn't to domesticate inspiration—it's to give it somewhere to land. Without such containers, our energy can dissipate in endless possibility. With too much containment, we suffocate our imagination. Rituals maintain the living tension between these forces.

The Power of Small Rhythms

The most transformative rituals are often simple: lighting a candle before writing, walking at sunset to signal closure, pausing before meals to breathe. These small, repetitive acts carve out sacred space in ordinary time. They help us remember that meaning isn't found only in great achievements but in the quiet choreography of our days.

When we design our own rituals—ones that feel alive rather than imposed—we cultivate autonomy and renewal. Our nervous system learns the difference between striving and settling. This balance restores creative clarity.

A day without ritual can dissolve into noise; a life with too much ritual can become mechanical. The art lies in keeping the practice fresh, allowing it to evolve as we do.

Rituals Across Seasons

Human creativity follows cycles, much like nature. There are seasons for planting ideas, seasons for incubation, and seasons for harvest. Recognizing these rhythms prevents burnout. For instance:

- **Spring rituals** might involve clearing space, setting intentions, and embracing novelty.
- **Summer rituals** could focus on energy and expression—working longer, taking bold steps.

- **Autumn rituals** might center on reflection, refinement, or gratitude.
- **Winter rituals** invite rest, silence, and integration.

When we align with such natural cycles, we stop fighting our fluctuating energy. We allow ebb and flow to guide us instead of resisting it. This alignment keeps our creative equilibrium alive.

Practice: Design One Ritual of Renewal

Choose one moment in your day that tends to blur or drain you—perhaps the end of work, the transition from one project to another, or the start of your morning. Design a ritual that helps you cross that threshold with intention.

Examples:

- **End-of-day ritual:** Write down three things you completed, close your laptop, and light a small candle for five minutes as a symbolic boundary between work and life.
- **Creative entry ritual:** Brew a specific tea, stretch, and play a short instrumental track before sitting down to create.

The goal isn't to perform perfection—it's to mark transitions. When you do, the mind learns to return to center, and the creative cycle renews itself naturally.

4.3 – Dynamic Balance in Real Time

Balance is not a static condition—it's a living conversation. We often imagine equilibrium as standing still, holding everything in perfect proportion. But true balance is more like surfing, dancing, or breathing: constant micro-adjustments to shifting conditions.

In life, we oscillate between expansion and contraction, focus and rest, control and surrender. Trying to freeze balance is like trying to trap a river in a jar—it stops flowing. The art is to move *with* the current, not against it.

The Myth of Static Harmony

We're often taught to "find balance" as though it's a destination: a stable arrangement of time, energy, and emotion. But any fixed balance is temporary because life itself moves. New demands arise, passions flare, fatigue sets in, and relationships evolve. Instead of clinging to symmetry, we can practice awareness—sensing when one side of the scale is tipping and adjusting with compassion rather than judgment.

Static balance leads to brittleness. Dynamic balance cultivates adaptability. It's the difference between a tightrope walker frozen mid-step and one who flows across, aware of every wobble but unafraid of it.

Negotiating Balance Moment by Moment

Dynamic balance means learning to listen—to the body, to time, to context. When energy wanes, rest isn't laziness but wisdom. When inspiration strikes, structure isn't rigidity but support. The practice is not about equal distribution but right relationship: knowing when to yield and when to assert, when to move forward and when to pause.

In real time, balance can look messy. One day's flow might mean deep focus; another's might mean stepping back entirely. The skill is to stay responsive rather than reactive. Awareness becomes our compass.

The Breath as a Teacher

Consider the breath: it expands and contracts continuously. You cannot hold your inhale or exhale forever. The moment you try, tension builds. The same is true of creative and emotional life. You need both inhalation (inspiration, rest, reflection) and exhalation (action, expression, engagement). To sustain creative equilibrium, honor both cycles.

Whenever you feel imbalanced, notice your breath. Are you metaphorically holding it—trying to freeze a perfect state? Or are you allowing it to move, trusting that stability arises through motion?

Reflection Prompt: Letting Balance Breathe

Ask yourself:

- Where in your life am I trying to *freeze* balance instead of letting it evolve?
- What would it look like to trust motion over maintenance?
- Which parts of my routine, work, or relationships need more flexibility—and which need firmer roots?

Journal on these questions. Let your answers be fluid. You may discover that balance is not something to "keep," but something to *keep rediscovering*.

Integrating Creative Equilibrium

To live at the intersection of chaos and order is to embrace life as an improvisation. You can plan the melody, but the rhythm comes from what's unfolding around you. Creative equilibrium doesn't mean avoiding extremes—it means learning to play between them.

When you lean too far into order, you may feel safe but uninspired. When you lean too far into chaos, you may feel free but untethered. Both are invitations: order reminds you to build structure; chaos reminds you to stay alive within it.

The balance you seek is not external—it's a dialogue between inner stability and outer change. This dialogue deepens through three enduring practices:

1. **Trust the edge:** Discomfort is not always a warning—it's often an invitation. When uncertainty appears, ask what new capacity is trying to emerge.
2. **Renew through rhythm:** Rituals keep creativity sustainable. They mark beginnings and endings, ensuring that chaos has form and order has flow.
3. **Move dynamically:** Balance is motion, not symmetry. Let your creative life breathe like lungs—constantly expanding and contracting.

Ultimately, equilibrium is a relationship with motion. You won't find it once and for all; you will *practice* it daily. The edge will shift. The balance will wobble. The ritual will evolve. That's the beauty of it—it's alive, just like you.

Closing Reflection: The Symphony of Change

Imagine your life as an orchestra tuning before a performance. There's noise, dissonance, half-finished sounds. Then, slowly, the tones align—not into perfection, but into readiness. The conductor raises the baton. That's the moment of equilibrium—not when the music is flawless, but when everything is poised for creation.

Creative equilibrium is not the end of chaos or the triumph of order. It's the ongoing act of tuning yourself to life's changing key. Each day offers a new tempo, a new note to play. Your task is not to silence the noise, but to make music with it.

Chapter 5 — The Long Horizon: Crafting a Future You Can Grow Into

A long horizon is more than a timeline—it is a philosophy of becoming. It is the understanding that who you are now is not a fixed endpoint but a starting place for expansion. A long horizon is what allows us to build with patience, to dream without panic, and to design our lives as ecosystems rather than projects. To live with a long horizon is to understand that time is not an enemy to be outrun, but a companion to be walked with. It invites a new kind of ambition—one that is slower, deeper, and more resilient.

In this chapter, we will explore three interwoven principles that help shape a life that matures gracefully over time:

1. **Patience as Power** — how to transform patience from passive endurance into active trust in your process.
2. **Designing a Legacy Loop** — how to redefine legacy as a living ripple rather than a static monument.
3. **Becoming Your Own Teacher** — how to create an internal ecosystem of learning that frees you from dependence on approval or praise.

The long horizon is not about waiting for a better future—it's about becoming the kind of person who can inhabit that future when it arrives.

5.1 – Patience as Power

In a world addicted to immediacy, patience is often misunderstood. We associate it with stagnation or weakness, as though waiting means doing nothing. But true patience is not passive; it is an act of trust in the unfolding of time and in your own growth. Patience, in its highest form, is a disciplined refusal to panic when progress isn't visible yet.

The Misunderstanding of Waiting

Most people think of waiting as absence—a gap between where you are and where you want to be. But waiting, when done consciously, is actually presence. It is the art of remaining faithful to the process even when the outcome hides from view. Impatience, on the other hand, comes from distrust—distrust that your effort will pay off, that your growth will continue, that time will not betray you.

When impatience drives you, you start grabbing for shortcuts. You push the seed into bloom before its roots can take hold. You rush to "arrive," but arrival without depth always collapses back into confusion. Patience, by contrast, builds from the inside out. It says: *I don't need proof yet, because I know what I'm building.* It replaces anxiety with alignment.

Active Patience: A New Definition

Patience is not idleness—it is the most strategic form of persistence. Active patience means working with full engagement *without demanding immediate results*. It's the posture of a gardener: tending the soil daily, trusting that growth happens invisibly before it shows above ground.

In a practical sense, active patience looks like:

- **Staying consistent** with your habits even when results are slow.
- **Delaying unnecessary comparison**—not measuring your Chapter 2 against someone else's Chapter 10.
- **Choosing depth over speed**—refining your craft rather than chasing applause.

Patience is power because it allows compound growth to work in your favor. What feels slow in the moment often turns out to be exponential in the long view.

Trusting Time

Patience becomes transformative when it merges with trust—not in fate, but in the integrity of your effort. When you know that your energy is well-placed, you can stop obsessing over when the reward will come. This trust allows creative tension to build; it creates a kind of psychological spaciousness that gives your ideas and abilities room to mature.

Every meaningful pursuit requires this trust. Relationships, art, business, health, mastery—all of them demand the ability to move forward without knowing exactly when things will "click." The long horizon is where patience and trust converge.

Exercise: The Shortcuts Audit

Think of one goal or project where impatience has driven your behavior. Maybe it's a skill you want to master, a business you want to grow, or a personal transformation you've been chasing. Ask yourself:

1. What shortcuts have I taken out of fear that it was "taking too long"?
2. What did those shortcuts cost me in depth, learning, or authenticity?
3. If I chose patience instead of panic, how might my process change this week?

Then, make one concrete adjustment. Maybe you slow down your pace, refocus on fundamentals, or release the pressure to prove something. Let your patience become a quiet declaration: *I trust the work I'm doing.*

5.2 – Designing a Legacy Loop

Legacy is often misunderstood as something that begins after we're gone. But true legacy is not posthumous—it's continuous. It's the ripple of your influence in motion right now, shaped by the way you live, listen, and lead.

The legacy loop is the ongoing feedback between what you give and what you grow from. It's the understanding that every interaction, project, and choice becomes part of a cycle that shapes both you and others. Legacy, then, is less about *what you leave behind* and more about *what you set in motion.*

Rethinking Legacy: From Achievement to Essence

When people talk about legacy, they often think in terms of trophies, titles, or tangible outcomes. But achievements decay. What endures is the energy we transfer—the courage, curiosity, and care we leave in others. That is the living essence of legacy.

To design a legacy loop, start by asking not, *What do I want to be remembered for?* but rather, *What do I want to multiply in others?* This shift transforms legacy from an ego project into a relational one. It turns your life into an open-source blueprint—something that evolves and expands through those you influence.

Legacy as a Living System

Legacy, when designed consciously, is a feedback system between contribution and reflection. Every time you teach, share, or help, you create ripples that come back to shape you. Those ripples refine your understanding, your empathy, and your craft.

This loop keeps you from stagnation. Instead of reaching a "final version" of yourself, you stay in dynamic evolution—constantly learning from the impact you create.

To maintain a healthy legacy loop:

- **Give intentionally**—offer your time, knowledge, and attention where they can genuinely enrich others.
- **Listen deeply**—allow feedback from those ripples to inform your next growth phase.
- **Evolve generously**—let your growth feed back into your giving.

When you live this way, your influence becomes renewable. You are not leaving a static legacy; you are curating a growing one.

Sustainability of Legacy

A sustainable legacy is one that others can build upon without your direct involvement. This means designing systems, habits, and values that are transferable. It could be mentoring someone in a skill, creating tools that help others grow, or modeling emotional intelligence that normalizes self-awareness in your circle.

Your legacy loop strengthens each time someone you've influenced passes that influence forward. This is how the long horizon stretches beyond your individual lifetime—it becomes an intergenerational conversation about meaning and mastery.

Reflection Prompt: The Three Qualities Test

Take a quiet moment and write down three qualities—not achievements—that you want to leave in others. Think of the kind of energy, awareness, or courage you want to plant, not the resume line you hope to earn.

For example:

- *Resilience* — so they know how to endure and rebuild.
- *Integrity* — so they can act from alignment even when unseen.
- *Curiosity* — so they continue asking better questions, long after I'm gone.

Next, for each quality, identify one daily behavior that nurtures it. Legacy is not built in the future; it's woven through the present.

5.3 – Becoming Your Own Teacher

At some point, every mature creator, leader, or learner must face this question: *Who teaches you once you've outgrown your mentors?* The answer, if you are to sustain lifelong growth, must eventually be: *I do.*

Becoming your own teacher is not about rejecting external wisdom—it's about learning to generate insight from within. It's the ability to extract lessons from every experience, whether it feels like success or failure. It's the skill of translating observation into growth without needing validation from others.

The Shift from Approval to Reflection

Most of us are trained from childhood to seek feedback as a measure of worth. Grades, promotions, likes, and applause all shape our understanding of success. But external feedback, while useful, is limited—it often mirrors conformity, not truth.

To become your own teacher, you must cultivate an inner feedback loop that is reflective, honest, and compassionate. Instead of asking, *Did I do it right?* you begin asking, *What did I learn? What did this teach me about how I work, lead, or create?*

Reflection becomes your curriculum. Every week, every project, every conversation becomes a lesson if you know how to listen inwardly.

Building a Lifelong Feedback System

A lifelong feedback system has three layers:

1. **Observation:** Paying attention to what happens without judgment. This is noticing patterns in behavior, emotion, or results.
2. **Interpretation:** Asking what these patterns reveal about your assumptions, skills, or fears.
3. **Integration:** Turning insight into adjusted action. Reflection without application is inertia; integration completes the learning cycle.

Over time, this system becomes second nature. You stop needing to be told what to fix—you learn to sense it. You stop fearing mistakes—you learn to mine them.

The Courage to Self-Correct

Self-teaching demands courage. It requires that you face your blind spots without self-condemnation. It's not about being your harshest critic but your most committed student. You learn to meet your missteps with curiosity rather than shame, asking, *What is this moment trying to teach me that success could not?*

The more you practice this, the freer you become. You no longer depend on approval to feel progress; your growth becomes self-sustaining.

Practice: The Weekly Reflection Triad

At the end of each week, set aside 15 minutes to complete this exercise. In your journal, answer three questions:

1. **From Success:** What went right this week, and what does it reveal about my strengths or alignment?
2. **From Failure:** What went wrong, and what hidden lesson or redirection might it contain?
3. **From Observation:** What did I learn from watching others—something I admired, or something I wish to avoid?

This simple triad builds an ongoing archive of learning. Over months, you'll start to see patterns—recurring lessons that shape your philosophy and refine your decision-making. This is how you become your own teacher, step by step, insight by insight.

The Architecture of a Long Horizon Life

When you weave together patience, legacy, and self-teaching, you create a powerful ecosystem of growth. Each principle reinforces the others:

- **Patience** gives you endurance for the long arc.
- **Legacy** gives your effort meaning beyond yourself.
- **Self-teaching** ensures you keep evolving as your context changes.

Together, they form a dynamic structure that scales with time instead of collapsing under it. You stop rushing toward a finish line and start building a rhythm of continuous evolution.

The Long Horizon Mindset

Living with a long horizon means you no longer measure success by speed, visibility, or applause. Instead, you measure it by alignment—whether your actions today move in rhythm with your deepest values.

You begin to understand that greatness is not the result of intensity but of *duration*. Most things worth building take longer than expected—but they also last longer than imagined. The long horizon asks you to trade immediacy for maturity, and noise for depth.

This mindset turns time into an ally. It softens urgency into rhythm, anxiety into trust, and ambition into stewardship. You begin to see that your life's work is not a race but a garden, and your job is to keep planting.

Bringing It All Together: Living the Long Horizon

To craft a future you can grow into, consider these guiding principles:

1. **Build from conviction, not comparison.** Patience frees you from the need to keep up; your timeline is your teacher.
2. **Design ripples, not monuments.** Legacy is not about being remembered—it's about keeping something alive through others.
3. **Learn to learn.** The world will always change faster than your plans. Reflection is your built-in navigation system.

The long horizon is not about deferring joy or ambition. It's about anchoring them so deeply that they can survive storms. It's about holding both urgency and eternity in the same hand—the drive to grow, and the wisdom to wait.

You will outgrow versions of yourself. You will rebuild again and again. But through it all, patience will give you power, your legacy loop will give you purpose, and your self-teaching will give you freedom.

And perhaps that is the ultimate art of a long horizon life: to build something that keeps teaching you how to live.

Printed in Dunstable, United Kingdom